PRESENTED TO

....

BY

....

DATE

....

The Early Reader's Bible
Copyright © 1991 by V. Gilbert Beers
Revised edition, copyright © 1995 by V. Gilbert Beers
Illustrations copyright © 1995 by Terri Steiger

Requests for information should be addressed to:
Zonderkidz, *Grand Rapids, Michigan 49530*

Library of Congress Cataloging-in-Publication Data

Beers, V. Gilbert (Victor Gilbert), 1928–
    The early reader's Bible / as told by V. Gilbert Beers;
    Illustrations by Terri Steiger. Includes index.
       p. cm.
    "63 easy-to-read Bible selections, each with story text and activity page."
    ISBN 978-0-310-70139-2
    1. Bible stories, English. [1. Bible stories.] I. Steiger, Terri, ill. IITitle
    2. BS551.2B432 1991
    3. 220.9'505–dc20

Zonderkidz is a trademark of Zondervan.

Printed in China

A Bible to Read All by Yourself!

The
Early Reader's
Bible

As told by V. Gilbert Beers

Illustrations by Terri Steiger

ZONDERVAN.com/
AUTHORTRACKER
follow your favorite authors

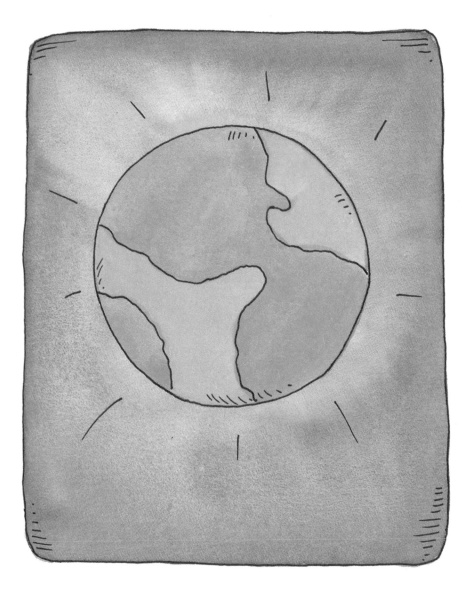

God Made Many Things

Creation, from Genesis 1-2

Long ago there was no world.

There was no sun.

There was no moon.

There were no stars.

"I will make a world," God said.

So God made our world.

"I will make a sun," God said.

So God made the sun.

Then God said, "It is a good sun.

It helps you see all day long."

"Now I will make a moon," God said.

"And I will make stars."

So God made the moon and the stars.

"They are good," said God.

"They help you see at night."

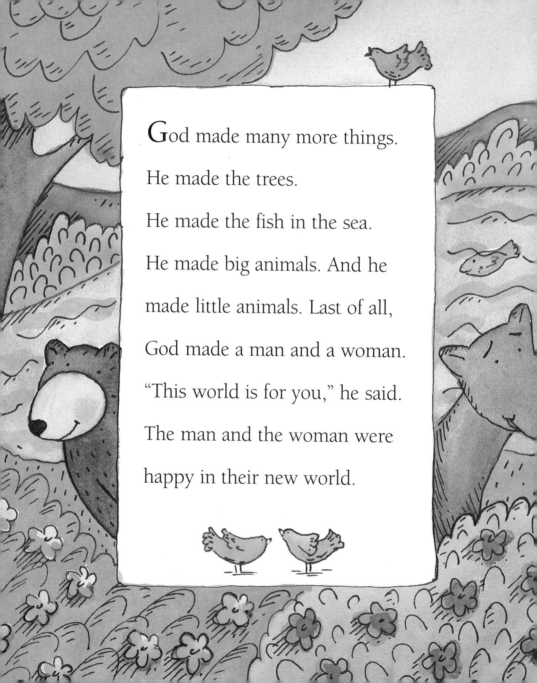

God made many more things.

He made the trees.

He made the fish in the sea.

He made big animals. And he made little animals. Last of all, God made a man and a woman.

"This world is for you," he said.

The man and the woman were happy in their new world.

something to ask

1. Who made the world?

2. Who made the sun, moon, and stars?

3. Who made the animals?

4. Are you happy God made all of these?

5. Have you thanked him?

something to do

When you see the moon, thank God for it.

When you see the stars, thank God for them.

And thank God for other good things too.

Something Bad, Something Sad

Adam and Eve's Temptation, from Genesis 3

Adam was Eve's husband.

Eve was Adam's wife.

They had a good home. They had good food.

They had many good things.

And they were never sad.

But there was one thing they could not have.

"You must not eat the food on that tree,"

God said.

11

For a time, Adam and Eve did not eat from it.

Then Satan talked to Eve one day.

"It is good," he said. "You should eat some."

Eve knew that God did not want her to eat

from that tree.

But the food looked good.

And Satan said it was good.

So Eve ate some.

Adam ate some, too.

Then Adam and Eve knew that they

had done something bad.

God was sad.

"You ate the food I told you not to eat," he said.

"Now you must go away from your home. Now you must work for your food."

Adam and Eve were sad, too.

"We should have done what God told us to do," they said.

something to ask

1. Have you done some things that you should not do?

2. Did these things please God?

3. Did Adam and Eve please God?

4. Why should you try to please God in all you do?

something to do

How do you know when something is bad?

When it makes
others sad.

When God says
it is bad.

When Mother and
Father say it is bad.

When you know that
you should not do it.

Noah Makes a Big Boat

The Flood and the Ark, from Genesis 6-7

"Make a big boat," God said.

"Yes," said Noah. "I will."

Noah loved God. Noah obeyed God.

He wanted to do what God said.

God told Noah how to make the boat.

Noah made it like God said.

It took a long time.

Noah put many animals
on the boat.

Then Noah went into the boat.

His family went with him.

One day it began to rain.

It rained and rained and rained.

Then it rained some more.

The water went over the houses.

It went over the trees.

The water went higher and higher and higher.

Soon there were no more people.

But Noah and his family were in the boat.

Noah had obeyed God.

So God took care of Noah.

"Thank you, God," Noah said one day.

Noah thanked God for taking care of him.

He thanked God for taking care of his family.

He thanked God for taking care of the animals.

something to ask

1. Who takes care of you?

2. Have you thanked your mother and father?

3. Have you thanked God?

4. Have you thanked others?

something to do

Here are some ways to say thanks:

Say thank you to others.

Do something good for others.

Tell others that you love them.

A Time to Say Thank You

Noah Worships God, from Genesis 8

There was water over all the world.

But Noah and his family did not get hurt.

God had told Noah to make a big boat.

He told Noah to take his family on the big boat.

He told Noah to take many animals, too.

God was taking care of them all.

They were in the boat for many days.

One day Noah looked out of the big boat.

The water was all gone.

God had taken it away.

"We must thank God for helping us," said Noah.

Noah and his family said thank you to God.

God was pleased. He made a

rainbow for them to see.

"The rainbow will tell you about

my promise," God said.

"I will not send water over all

the world anymore."

Noah was happy to hear God's

promise. He was happy that he

had said thank you to God!

something to ask

1. How did Noah thank God?

2. Why did he do this?

3. What did God do then?

4. How can you thank God for the good
   things he has done for you?

something to do

Do you thank God for...

God's house?   Your house?

Your food?   Mother and Father?

Your things?
Your friends?
Others in your family?

A Promise for Abraham

A Son for Abraham and Sarah, Genesis 18 and 21

Abraham and Sarah loved God.

They prayed to God.

They wanted to please God.

God loved Abraham and Sarah, too.

He gave them many good things.

But there was one thing Abraham and Sarah

did not have. They did not have a son.

One night God said to Abraham,

"Try to count the stars."

Abraham saw many, many stars.

He could not count them all.

"Your family will be like the stars,"

said God. "I will give you a son.

Your son will have children.

And some day your family

will be too big to count."

After a long time, Sarah had a baby boy.

"God did what he promised to do," said Abraham.

"God gave us this baby boy."

Abraham and Sarah gave their boy a name.

"We will call him Isaac," they said.

How happy they were with their baby boy!

And God was happy, too.

something to ask

1. How did Abraham and Sarah show that they loved God?

2. How can you show that you love God?

3. What did God promise Abraham and Sarah?

4. Did God do what he promised?

5. What are some of God's promises to you?

6. Do you think that God will do what he promised?

something to do

When is a good time to think about

God's promises?

At night

When you play

When you are sad

When you are happy

Jacob Sees a Ladder

Jacob's Dream, from Genesis 27-28

words to know

Jacob
angel
dream
ladder
heaven

Jacob was very sad.

He had to go away from home.

He had to go far away.

So Jacob walked all day.

He walked far from home.

When it was night he stopped.

43

One night Jacob had a dream.

He saw a ladder.

It went all the way to heaven.

Angels went up and down

on the ladder.

Then God talked to Jacob.

"I will go with you," God said.

"I will help you."

Jacob stopped dreaming.

He sat up.

"God was here," he said.

"And God will go with me."

Jacob was happy.

He wanted God to go with him.

He wanted God to help him.

something to ask

1. What did Jacob see?

2. Where did the ladder go?

3. Who was on the ladder?

4. Who talked to Jacob?

5. What did God say?

6. Why was Jacob happy?

something to do

Is God with you?

Would you like him to be with you?

Will you ask him now?

God Takes Care of Joseph

Joseph in Egypt, from Genesis 37-41

Joseph's brothers did not like him.

They wanted to hurt him.

Let's kill Joseph," said one brother.

"No," said another brother.

"Let's sell him. He will be a slave.

He will have to work and work and work."

Joseph's brothers DID sell him.

But God took care of Joseph.

Then something bad happened.

A man put Joseph in jail.

But God took care of Joseph.

One night the king had a dream.

"What does the dream mean?" the king asked.

No one could tell him.

"Joseph can tell you," said a man.

He had been in jail with Joseph.

The king sent for Joseph.

"I will tell you what your
dream means," Joseph said.
So he told the king.
The king was very happy.
"You are a good man," he said.
"I will put you over my people."
So the king put Joseph over
all the people.
God was taking care of Joseph.

something to ask

1. How did Joseph's brothers hurt him?

2. How did God take care of Joseph?

3. How does God take care of you?

4. Do you ask God to do this?

something to do

Write ASK on some paper.

Put it where you can see it each day.

When you see ASK, ask God to help you.

Joseph Forgives His Brothers

Joseph and His Brothers Reunited, from Genesis 42-45

Joseph's brothers had been mean to him.

They sold him, so Joseph became a slave.

But God took care of Joseph.

He helped Joseph tell the king about his dream.

So the king put Joseph over all his people.

One day Joseph's brothers
came to see him.
They did not know that he
was Joseph.
Joseph's brothers wanted to
buy grain.
Joseph sold them grain
to take home.

After many days they came back.

They wanted to buy more grain.

Then Joseph told them who he was.

Joseph's brothers were afraid.

They thought Joseph would kill them.

But he did not want to do that.

"I forgive you," said Joseph.

This pleased God.

God wants us to forgive others.

He forgives us, too.

something to ask

1. What did Joseph's brothers do to him?

2. Were they mean to Joseph?

3. Did Joseph forgive his brothers?

4. Do you think that pleased God?

something to do

Which word is not here?

Joseph wanted to _____ his brothers.

God wants to _____ you.

(Turn this over to see the word.)

Miriam Is a Brave Girl

words to know

Miriam
basket
brave
river
princess

The Baby Moses in the Basket, from Exodus 2

The king did not like Miriam's people.

He wanted to kill all their baby boys.

"The king's men must not find our baby,"

said Miriam's mother.

"But where can we put him?

If we put him in our house

the king's men will find him.

Miriam's mother made a basket.

"We will put him in this," she said.

Then she put the basket on the river.

"I will stay with our baby," said Miriam.

She was a brave girl.

Soon a woman came to the river to wash.

She was the princess.

"A basket!" the princess said to her helpers.

"Go get it for me."

The princess looked in the basket.

She said, "I will keep this baby.

But I want someone to take care of him."

Miriam ran to the princess.

"I know someone who
will do it," she said.

"My mother will take care of him."

Miriam's mother was so happy.

The king's men could not hurt
her baby now.

She said, "Thank you, Miriam,
for being my brave helper."

something to ask

1. What did the king want to do?

2. What did Miriam do that was brave?

3. How can you be like Miriam?

something to do

When should you be brave?

Who can help you be brave?

God Talks to Moses

Moses and the Burning Bush, from Exodus 2-4

The princess found a baby in a basket.

She named him Moses.

Moses was now a man.

He lived in Egypt.

But the king wanted to kill him,

so he ran away.

Moses took care of his sheep

far away from his home.

75

Moses looked at his sheep.

"My sheep are happy," he said.

"But my people are not happy.

They are slaves."

Then Moses saw a bush.

It was burning. But it did not burn up.

God talked to Moses from the bush.

"Go back to Egypt," God said.

"Lead my people away from there.

They must not work for the king anymore."

Moses did not want to do this.

He was afraid of the

king of Egypt.

But Moses obeyed God.

He went to Egypt.

He would lead God's people

away from there.

He would do what God wanted

him to do.

something to ask

1. What did Moses see?

2 What did God tell Moses to do?

3. Why was Moses afraid? What
   did the king want to do?

4. Why did Moses go back to Egypt?

5. What would he do there?

something to do

Who should you obey?

Mother?

Father?

God?

Bad friends?

A King Who Said No

Pharaoh and Moses, from Exodus 5-12

"Let God's people go!" said Moses.

"Stop making them do your work."

"No!" said the king.

"God says you must," said Moses.

"But I do not do what your God tells me,"

the king said.

Time after time Moses talked
to the king.
But the king would not do what
God said.
"No," the king said.
The king made God's people do
all his work.
They did not get much rest.
They did not get much to eat.

Then God told Moses what to do.

"Go back to the king.

Tell him to let my people go

or bad things will happen."

But the king did not obey God.

So God hurt the king and he

hurt the king's people.

The king was afraid.

He said, "Take your people and go away!"

So Moses and his people went to a new home.

They went far from the king who said no to God.

something to ask

1. What did Moses want the king to do?

2. Why did the king say no?

3. What made the king say yes?

4. How can you say yes to God?

something to do

Who is saying no to God here?

I will not talk to
God now.

I want to go to
God's house.

I will not do what
Mother says.

Please tell me
about Jesus.

Going Out of Egypt

The Exodus, from Exodus 13-15

God's people went away from Egypt.

They went as fast as they could go.

Moses led them.

The people knew that God was with them.

Each day, in a cloud, God was with the people.

Each night the cloud was like fire.

God was with the people all the time.

He was showing them where to go.

One day the people came to a big sea.

They could not go over it.

They could not go around it.

The king and his men were coming fast.

They wanted to kill God's people.

But God made a dry place to walk in the sea.

On one side the water was high.

On the other side the water was high.

But there was a dry place

where the people could walk.

Moses led the people through the sea.

The king and his men came, too.

But God made the sea go
over them.

God took care of his people.

He helped Moses lead them away

from Egypt. They were not the

king's slaves anymore.

So they sang a happy song.

something to ask

1. Why did the people want to go away from Egypt?

2. Who led them?

3. How did the people know that God was with them?

4. How did they get across the sea?

5. Did God take care of them?
   How do you know?

something to do

God took care of the people.

So they sang a song for him.

Does God take care of you?

Will you sing a happy song for him?

Something to Drink, Something to Eat

Water and Manna in the Wilderness, from Exodus 15-16

"I want some water," a little girl said.

"We want water, too," said her father.

"But there is no water.

We are not slaves in Egypt now.

But we cannot find water."

Then someone ran fast.

"Water!" he said. "I see water!"

99

All the people went to get

some water.

But they could not drink it.

It was not good water.

"Cut down that tree," God said,

"and put it into the water."

Moses did what God said.

Now the water was

good to drink.

"I want something to eat," a little boy said.

"We want something to eat, too," said his mother.

"But there is no food."

"God will give you food," said Moses.

So God sent birds for the people to eat.

He sent bread each day. It was called manna.

Their food was not like our food.

But it was good food.

God gave it to his people.

That is how God took care of his people.

something to ask

1. Why was there no food or water?

2. How did God make the bad water become good water?

3. What kind of bread did God send? What was it called?

4. What other food did God send?

something to do

Look in your house. Ask your mother to help you.

How many kinds of food can you find?

How many kinds did God's people have?

Will you thank God for your good food?

God's Good Rules

The Ten Commandments, from Exodus 19-20

"What is it?" some people asked.

"Thunder!" some said.

"Lightning!" others said.

The people were near a big mountain.

They were afraid.

But Moses was there with them.

God had helped Moses lead the people.

He had helped Moses take them to this place.

God told Moses to go up

on the mountain.

Moses obeyed God.

He wanted to hear what God

would say.

God talked with Moses.

He gave Moses some good rules.

He said, "Tell my people to obey

these rules."

These are God's good rules:

1. Worship only God.

2. Do not make something and think it is God.

3. Do not say God's name in a bad way.

4. Rest on God's day.

5. Love and obey your mother and father.

6. Do not kill people.

7. Love your wife or husband.

8. Do not steal.

9. Do not lie.

10. Do not want what others have.

something to ask

1. What good rules did God give Moses?

2. Should you obey these rules, too?

3. Who will you please if you obey
   these rules?

something to do

God told Moses and his people what he wanted.

He talked to Moses.

How does God tell us now what he wants?

Where does he tell us what he wants?

A Calf of Gold

Israel Worships an Idol, from Exodus 32

"Will you do what God says?"

Moses asked.

"Yes," said the people.

"We will do what God says."

Moses went away.

He went to talk with God.

Moses was gone for a long time.

"Moses will not come back," some people said.

"We must have someone to help us."

So the people made a calf from gold.

"This gold calf will help us," they said.

"It will be our god now."

But the people were not doing what God said.

They were not pleasing God.

One day Moses came back.

He did not like what the people were doing.

"Do you want to please God?" he asked.

"Come here!"

The people who wanted to
please God came to Moses.
But some would not come.
Then something happened to
the bad people.
The bad people died.
It was a sad day for the people
who said no to God.

something to ask

1. What did the people do that was bad?

2. How did God like their gold calf?

3. Is God not happy about some things you do?

4. What should you do about these things?

something to do

When should you do what God wants?

Some of the time?

All of the time?

None of the time?

God's People Are Sorry

The Bronze Serpent, from Numbers 21

words to know

snake
brass
sorry
angry
punish

"Why did you lead us here?"

some people said to Moses.

"We do not like our food."

Others said, "God does not help us."

Moses was sad to hear these things.

God's people were not slaves in Egypt now.

God had helped Moses lead his people here.

He had given them good food.

123

But the people wanted better food and a better place.

They did not want to please God.

So God sent snakes to punish his people.

"Run!" said the people.

But the people could not run away from the snakes.

The people came to Moses.

"Help us!" they said.

Moses talked to God about this.

"Make a big brass snake," God told Moses.

"Put it up high for the people to see.

People who look at it will not die."

Moses did what God told him to do.

The people who looked at the snake did not die.

That was a way to say they were sorry.

Then God would help them.

He would forgive them.

something to ask

1. What did the people want?

2. Why was God angry about that?

3. How did God punish them?

4. How could the people say they were sorry?

something to do

Put BAD, SORRY, and PRAY on some paper.

Put this where you will see it each day.

When you do something bad, look at it.

Are you sorry? Then pray.

God Helps Joshua

The Walls of Jericho, from Joshua 6

"Look at those walls," said God's people.

"How can we fight the people of Jericho?

How can we get over those walls?"

"God will help us," said Joshua.

God DID help Joshua.

He told Joshua how to fight Jericho.

Then Joshua told the people.

This is the way they did it.

Joshua and the people went
around the walls of Jericho.
Then they went home.
The next day they went
around the walls again.
They did this each day.
"What are they doing?"
asked the people of Jericho.
"Why don't they fight us?"

One day Joshua and the people

went around and around the walls.

They went around the walls seven times.

Then they stopped.

The people of Jericho were afraid.

What would happen now?

Joshua and the people began to shout.

The walls of Jericho fell down.

Joshua and the people ran into Jericho

and took it.

"God helped us do this," Joshua said.

something to ask

1. Who told Joshua how to take Jericho?

2. Did Joshua obey God?

3. How did Joshua take Jericho?

something to do

What would you like God to help you do?

Will you ask him to help you now?

A Man Made Strong by God

Samson, from Judges 13-16

Samson was the strongest man of all.

God had made him that way.

Samson was so strong that he killed a lion.

He did it with his hands.

Some people tried to kill Samson.

They did not like Samson's people.

But Samson was too strong for them.

Then Samson did some bad things.

He did things that did not please God.

He did things that did not please

his father and mother.

Samson did things that hurt him.

So God said, "Now Samson will not be strong."

Some people took Samson away.

Samson could not stop them.

The people made Samson work for them. They hurt him so that he could not see.

Then Samson was sad that he had not pleased God.

God had given Samson so much.

What do you think Samson should have done for God?

something to ask

1. Has God given you many good things?

2. What do you do for him?

3. What did Samson do?

4. What should you do that Samson did not do?

something to do

Who should do what God wants?

A New Family

Ruth Follows Naomi, from Ruth 1-4

"I am going home," Naomi said.

"I am going back to my people."

Many things had hurt Naomi.

Her husband had died.

Her sons had died.

Now she wanted to go back to her home.

"I will go with you," said Ruth.

So Ruth went back with Naomi to her people.

In their new home there was no one

to get food for Ruth and Naomi.

So Ruth went to look for food.

One day Ruth saw a good man.

His name was Boaz.

Boaz loved Ruth.

Ruth loved Boaz.

"May I be your husband?" Boaz asked Ruth.

Ruth was very happy.

She was happy to have Boaz

for her husband.

"Boaz will take care of Naomi

and me," she said.

"And he will love me, too."

After a time, Ruth and Boaz

had a baby boy.

They were a very happy family.

something to ask

1. Why was Ruth happy?

2. What can make a family happy?

3. Do you have a happy family?

4. What can you do to help your family?

5. Will this make you happy, too?

something to do

What is a family?

Do these things make a family?

What things DO make a family?

A Boy Gets a New Home

Samuel Dedicated to God, from 1 Samuel 1-2

Hannah wanted a baby so much.

So Hannah asked God for a baby boy.

"If you give me a little boy," said Hannah,

"I will let him do your work."

God did what Hannah asked.

Hannah was so happy with her baby boy.

"I will call him Samuel", she said.

"And I will give him to God."

When Samuel was bigger,

Hannah took him to God's house.

She talked to Eli, the man who took care of

God's house.

"Will you help my boy do God's work?"

Hannah asked.

"Yes," said Eli.

So Eli helped Samuel to know about God.

And Samuel helped Eli take care of God's house.

Samuel stayed with Eli

at God's house.

Hannah came to see him.

She took him many good things.

Samuel loved his mother.

He loved Eli, too.

And Samuel loved his new home

where he worked for God.

But best of all, he loved God.

something to ask

1. Where did Samuel live?

2. Why did he live there?

3. Why did Samuel love his new home?

4. How can you help God do his work?

something to do

When can you talk to God?

David Is a Brave Boy

David and Goliath, from 1 Samuel 17

"Come and fight me," Goliath called.

But not one of God's people would fight him.

They were afraid of Goliath.

A boy named David said,

"I am not afraid. I will fight Goliath."

"How can you?" asked the king.

"You are not as big as he is."

"God will help me," said David.

So David went to fight Goliath.

He took his sling.

And he took five stones.

The big man ran at David.

He wanted to kill David.

The people with Goliath wanted

to kill God's people, too.

David talked to God.

"Help me, God," he asked.

Then David put a stone in his
sling. Away went the stone.
Down went the big man!
The people with Goliath were
afraid. They ran away.
"David is brave," said the king.
David WAS brave.
But he knew that God had
helped him.

something to ask

1. What did Goliath want to do?

2. How did David show that he was brave?

3. What do you say to God when you
   need help?

something to do

What should you do when you don't feel brave?

Good Friends

David and Jonathan, from 1 Samuel 18

The king saw David kill Goliath.

He saw that David was a brave boy.

The king's son saw this, too.

His name was Jonathan.

He was a brave boy, too.

Jonathan wanted David to be his friend.

"Will you be my best friend?" Jonathan asked.

"Yes, I will be your best friend," said David.

Jonathan had many
good things.
He gave his best things
to David.
He gave David his sword.
He gave David his bow
and arrows.

He gave David his robe.

"This will show you that I am your friend,"

said Jonathan.

"Thank you for your best things," said David.

"And thank you for being my best friend."

something to ask

1. Who was Jonathan?

   Who was his father?

2. Why did Jonathan want to be
   David's friend?

3. What did Jonathan give David?

4. Why did he do this?

something to do

What should good friends do?

Fight each other?

Help each other?

Give each other
good things?

Say good things to
each other?

A Wise King

Solomon Judges Wisely, from 1 Kings 3

"Long live King Solomon!" the people said.

Solomon was the new king.

He was a very wise king.

He had asked God to make him wise.

One day two women came
with a baby.
Each woman said,
"This is MY baby!"
Solomon did not know who
was the mother.
"Cut the baby in two," he said
"Give some of it to each one."

"No!" said the mother.

"Yes!" said the other woman.

Then Solomon knew who the mother was.

"Give the baby to that woman," he said.

"How wise our king is," said the people.

"Thank you, God, for showing me what to do,"

said King Solomon.

something to ask

1. How did Solomon know what to do?

2. How did he show that he was wise?

3. Do you want someone to help you know what to do?

4. Who can help you?

5. Will you ask him?

something to do

What would God want you to do?

This...   or that?

This...   or that?

A Beautiful House for God

Solomon Builds the Temple, from 1 Kings 5-8

"What is King Solomon doing?" someone asked.

"He is building a house for God," said another.

"It will be very beautiful."

"Find the best trees for God's house," said the king.

"God's house must have the best trees of all."

So men went far away.

They cut the best trees.

Other men cut big stones for the walls.

Some worked with gold.

And some worked with cloth.

When people worked at God's
house, they were very quiet.
People worked for many days.
At last the work was done.
"Come see God's house,"
King Solomon told everyone.
"It is very beautiful!"
Many people came to see it.
"God is good!" they sang.

something to ask

1. What did King Solomon build?

2. Did Solomon build it with good things or bad things?

3. What did people do when God's house was done?

something to do

What should you do in God's house?

What should you NOT do?

Birds with Food for a Man

God Feeds Elijah, from 1 Kings 17

Elijah had to run away.

He had told the king what God said.

But the king did not like what God said.

He did not like to hear how bad he was.

So the king wanted to kill Elijah.

"You must hide from the king," God said.

"Where?" asked Elijah.

"I will show you," God said.

195

God showed Elijah

a little river.

"But what will I eat?"

Elijah asked.

There was no food

at the river.

So God gave Elijah food each day.

He sent birds with food for Elijah.

Now Elijah had good food to eat.

God gave it to him each day.

"Thank you," Elijah said.

"Thank you for giving me good food to eat."

something to ask

1. How did God give food to Elijah?

2. How does God give food to you?

3. Do you thank him for your good food?

4. Will you thank him now?

something to do

What food does God give you?

Elijah Helps a Family

Elijah and a Widow, from 1 Kings 17

No one had much food to eat.

There had been no rain for a long time.

So the food could not grow.

"Where will I get something to eat?" Elijah asked.

"I will show you," God said.

God told Elijah where to go.

It was a little town far away.

"You will find a woman there," God said.

"I will give her good food, and she will

give some to you."

Elijah went to the little town.

He found the woman.

But the woman had no food.

"Where will I get food for us?" she asked.

"God will give it to you," said Elijah.

205

God DID give the woman some
food for her family.

He gave her food for Elijah, too.

She was happy that Elijah came.

"You have helped us get good
food," the woman said.

"And you have helped me have
food, too," said Elijah.

something to ask

1. Where do Mother and Father get your food?

2. Who makes your food grow?

3. Can you make it grow?

4. Do you thank God for his help?

5. Will you thank him now?

something to do

How is God helping you get food?

A New Room

Elisha and the Woman from Shunem, from 2 Kings 4

"Please eat with us when you come this way,"

a man and woman told Elisha.

"You work for God. So we want to help you."

The man and woman could not work for God

the way Elisha did.

But they could give him something to eat.

They could help Elisha do God's work.

Elisha was happy to eat with them.

He knew they loved God as much as he did.

One day the woman had
a surprise for Elisha.
"Come with me," she said.
She took Elisha to a
beautiful room.
"We made this room for you,"
she said.
"Please stay here when you
come this way."

Elisha smiled as he looked at the room.

It was a beautiful place.

"Thank you," said Elisha.

"You put good things in the room for me."

"We are happy that you work for God,"

said the woman.

"And we are happy that we can help you

work for God."

something to ask

1. Who worked for God?

2. Who helped Elisha work for God?

3. How did they help him work for God?

something to do

You can help do God's work by sharing.

Which of these are ways to do this?

God Helps a Sick Man

Naaman and Elisha, from 2 Kings 5

Naaman went to see Elisha.

A friend went with him.

Naaman was very sick. He had leprosy.

Naaman wanted Elisha to help him.

Elisha talked to Naaman's friend.

He did not talk to Naaman.

"Tell Naaman to wash in the river,"

Elisha told Naaman's friend.

Naaman was angry.

He wanted to see Elisha.

He wanted Elisha to do something big.

He did not want to wash in Elisha's river.

So Naaman went away.

"Stop!" said Naaman's friend.

"Do what Elisha says."

So Naaman went back.

He washed in Elisha's river.

And what do you think

happened?

God made Naaman well again!

His leprosy went away because

he did what Elisha said.

something to ask

1. Who was sick? What sickness did he have?

2. What did Elisha tell him to do?

3. Why was Naaman angry?

4. What happened when Naaman obeyed Elisha?

something to do

Who should you obey?

Money to Fix God's House

Joash and the Money-Chest, from 2 Chronicles 24

King Joash loved God.

He wanted his people to love God, too.

He wanted his people to go to God's house.

But God's house was not

the happy house it should be.

People did not take good care of it.

"We must fix God's house," said the king.

"But we must have money to do that."

The king put a big box by God's house.

"Put your money in the box," said the king.

"Put money in there to fix God's house."

The people put their money in the box.

Soon the king had the money to fix God's house."

The people were pleased
that they could help.
They wanted to help fix
God's house.
Soon God's house was a
happy house.
And that is what God's
house should be!

something to ask

1. What did Joash want his people to do?

2. Why couldn't they do it?

3. What did Joash do to help God's house?

something to do

How can I help in God's house?

Building New Walls

Nehemiah in Jerusalem, from Nehemiah 1-8

Nehemiah worked for the king.

But one day Nehemiah looked sad.

"Why are you so sad?" the king asked.

"Long ago people tore down my city,"

Nehemiah said. "They tore down the walls."

"What do you want me to do?" the king asked.

"Please let me go home," said Nehemiah.

"Please let me build the walls again."

"You may go," said the king.

So Nehemiah went home.

He found some helpers.

They began to build the walls.

But some people did not like this.

They wanted to hurt Nehemiah.

They wanted to hurt his helpers.

They did not want Nehemiah's city

to have walls.

But Nehemiah was doing
something that God wanted
him to do.
So God helped Nehemiah build
the walls.
Nehemiah's friends came to
see the walls.
They thanked God for helping
Nehemiah.

something to ask

1. Why was Nehemiah sad?

2. What did he want to do?

3. What did the king tell him to do?

4. Why did Nehemiah's people thank God?

something to do

Find pictures of boys or girls who are helpers.

Ask Mother or Father to help you.

What are they doing?

Can you do these things, too?

Esther Is a Brave Queen

Esther Saves Her People, from Esther 1-10

A man came to see Queen Esther.

"Someone wants to kill our people,"

the man said.

"What can I do?" asked Queen Esther.

"Ask the king to help us," said the man.

But Esther could not do this.

She could not see the king

any time she wanted to see him.

243

"The king must ask me to see him,"

said Esther. "I could be killed."

Esther did not want to be killed.

But Esther loved her people.

So she went to see the king.

The king did not kill Esther.

He asked what he could do for her.

"Please help my people," said Queen Esther.

"A bad man wants to kill them.

He will kill me, too."

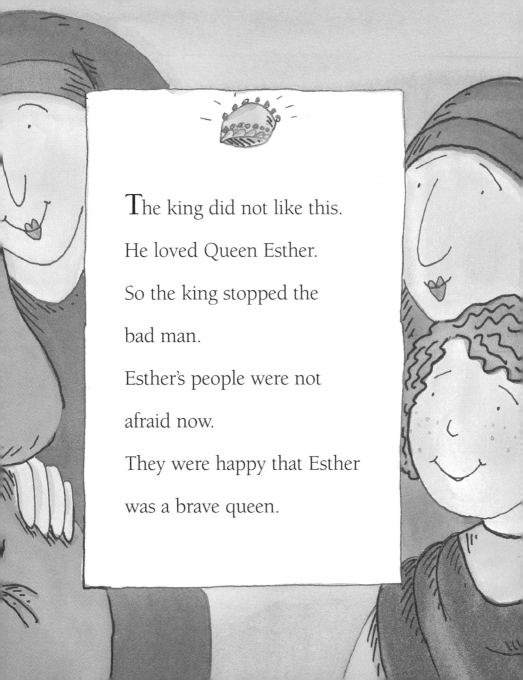

The king did not like this.

He loved Queen Esther.

So the king stopped the

bad man.

Esther's people were not

afraid now.

They were happy that Esther

was a brave queen.

something to ask

1. What did Esther do that was brave?

2. Why did she do this?

3. Who helped Esther to be brave?

4. How can God help you to be brave?

something to do

Who can help you to be brave?

Jesus?

Mother?

Father?

friends?

Job
learn
belong

Love God When You Hurt

Job's Suffering, from Job 1 and 42

Job was a good man who loved God.

So God gave him many good things.

One day something sad happened to Job.

A man ran up to him and said, "Job! Job!

Bad people took away some of your animals."

Then another man ran up to Job.

"Some of your other animals were killed," he said.

"And your helpers were killed, too."

251

Then another man ran up to Job.

"Your children were all killed," he said.

Job was so sad.

"God gave me these things," Job said.

"Then God took them from me.

But they belonged to God."

Then Job became sick.

Satan was doing all this to hurt Job.

He wanted Job to turn away from God.

But Job would not turn away
from God. He said,
"I will love God at all times."
God loved Job, too. He told
Satan to stop hurting Job.
God made Job well again.
He gave him a new family.
And he gave him many other
things, too.

something to ask

1. What did Satan do to Job?

2. Was Job sad? Did Job hurt?

3. Did Job turn away from God?

4. What do you do when you hurt?

5. Will God help you then?

something to do

Which of these will make you hurt?

When you are sick?

When Mother or Father is away?

When others do not like you?

When you cannot do something well?

When friends say bad things about you?

When you must have help?

What should you do then?

A Happy King

Daniel Interprets the King's Dream, from Daniel 2

words to know

means
Daniel

"I had a dream," said the king.

"But I do not know what it means."

"Tell me what I dreamed," he said to his men.

"Then tell me what will come from it."

"How can we tell you what you dreamed?"

the men said.

"If you do not tell me my dream," said

the king, "I will have someone kill you."

The king's men were afraid.

259

But Daniel was not afraid.

He said to the king, "I will tell

you about your dream."

Then Daniel talked to God

about the king's dream.

"Help me know what it is," he asked.

So God helped Daniel know

what the king's dream was about.

"Thank you, God," said Daniel. "Thank you

for telling me about the king's dream."

Then Daniel told the king about his dream.

The king was happy to know about the dream.

The king was kind to Daniel.

He gave Daniel many good things.

Then Daniel thanked God for his help.

something to ask

1. Why did Daniel talk to God about the king's dream?

2. What did God do for Daniel?

3. What should you say to God when he helps you?

4. Will you say it now?

something to do

Do you thank God at these times?

Daniel and the Lions

God Helps Daniel, from Daniel 6

"The king is going to put Daniel over us,"

some men said. They did not like this.

They wanted to be over Daniel.

So the men asked the king to make a bad rule.

"No one may ask any god for anything,"

the law said. "If he does, he will be

given to the lions to eat."

These men knew that Daniel talked to God.

They knew that he would ask God for help.

The men watched Daniel's house.

They saw Daniel talking to God.

So the men ran to tell the king.

The king liked Daniel.

He did not like what these men had done.

But the king had to let the men put Daniel
into the lion house. This was the law.

"Your God will help you," the king said.

The next day the king went

to the lion house.

"Did your God help you,

Daniel?" he asked.

"Yes," said Daniel.

"The lions did not hurt me."

The king was so happy.

Daniel was happy, too.

God had helped him.

something to ask

1. How did God help Daniel?

2. Why did Daniel talk to God when he hurt?

3. Why do you pray?

4. Do you pray each day?

something to do

What would stop you from praying?

A hungry lion?

A king?

Bad people?

Watching TV?

Jonah Learns to Obey

Jonah and the Fish, from Jonah 1-3

God sent a big storm.

Jonah was on a boat in the storm.

God had told Jonah to go to Nineveh.

Jonah did not want to go. So he ran away.

The other people on the boat were afraid.

Jonah said, "I am running away from God.

If you throw me into the water,

God will stop the storm."

The men threw Jonah into the water.

The storm stopped.

Then God sent a big fish.

God told the fish to swallow Jonah.

The big fish swallowed Jonah.

Jonah was in the fish for a long time.

There in the fish, Jonah prayed to God.

He told God he was sorry.

He asked God to forgive him.

Then God told the fish,

"Let Jonah go."

The fish obeyed God.

It threw Jonah out on the land.

Then God told Jonah to go to

Nineveh again.

This time Jonah obeyed.

He went and told the people

of Nineveh about God.

something to ask

1. Why did Jonah run away from God?

2. Where did God find him?

3. What did God do?

4. Why did Jonah go to Nineveh then?

something to do

Which words tell what Jonah did in the fish?

pray   sorry   angry   fight   forgive

Jesus Came to Love Us

Christ Is Born, from Luke 2 and Matthew 1

"You cannot stay here," the man said.

"I have all the people I can take."

"But where can we sleep?" Joseph asked.

"Mary is going to have a baby."

The man looked at his animals.

"You may sleep with them," he said.

"It is the only place I have."

So Mary and Joseph went to sleep with the animals.

That night Mary had a little baby.

"We will call him Jesus," Joseph said.

"That is what God said we should do."

"This baby is God's Son," said Mary.

"That is what God said."

"This baby has come to love us,"

said Mary and Joseph.

"And he has come to help us love God."

something to ask

1. Who was this little baby?

2. Why did he come?

3. Does Jesus love you?

4. Do you love Jesus?

something to do

How do you show Jesus that you love him?

Angels Sing to Shepherds

The Shepherds Visit Baby Jesus, from Luke 2

"Look at the sky," a shepherd said.

"It looks like it is day," said another.

"But it is night."

The shepherds were so afraid.

They did not know what it was.

"Don't be afraid," an angel said.

"I have something to tell you.

There is a new baby in town.

You should go to see him.

He is God's Son."

Then more angels came and

filled the sky.

They sang about God.

Then they went away.

"Let's go into town

and see the baby who is God's Son,"

the shepherds said.

They ran into town and went where

the angels said they should go.

How happy they were that they

could see baby Jesus!

They wanted to tell others about God's Son.

The shepherds told all the people they could find

about God's Son.

something to ask

1. Who did the shepherds see?

2. What did the angels tell the shepherds about Jesus?

3. What did the shepherds tell others?

4. Do you tell your friends about Jesus?

5. What do you tell them?

something to do

What do you tell others about Jesus?

He loves us.

He is my friend.

He wants to be your friend, too.

He wants you to live for him.

He will help you live in God's home in heaven.

What other things do you tell about Jesus?

The Wise Men Give Their Best

Gifts for Baby Jesus, from Matthew 2

"Look at the star," a wise man said.

"I see it," said another.

"We must follow that star.

It will take us to a new king."

The wise men knew that
this king was a special king.
He was only a little baby now.
But God had sent him.
The wise men went on camels.
They took their best gifts
to give to the baby king.
On and on they went for many
days, following the star.

One day the star stopped.

It stopped over the town of Bethlehem.

"This is the place," the wise men said.

"The baby king is here."

The wise men went to see Jesus.

They gave him their best gifts.

They were happy that the star

had led them to Jesus.

something to ask

1. What led the wise men to Jesus?

2. What did they give him?

3. Do you give Jesus your best gifts?

something to do

Which of these gifts can you give Jesus?

Jesus' Happy Family

The Childhood of Jesus, from Luke 2

"Will you help me?" Joseph asked.

Jesus was happy to help Joseph.

Joseph made many good things.

He made things from wood.

Joseph was a carpenter.

Jesus was a carpenter, too.

He helped Joseph make things from wood.

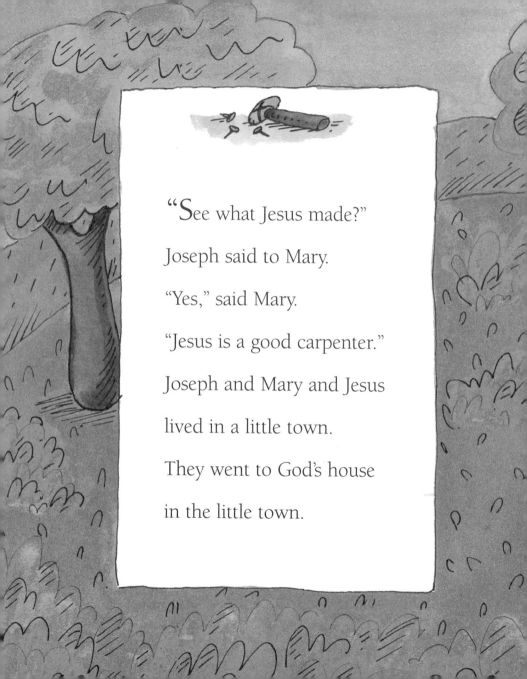

"See what Jesus made?"
Joseph said to Mary.

"Yes," said Mary.

"Jesus is a good carpenter."
Joseph and Mary and Jesus
lived in a little town.

They went to God's house
in the little town.

They liked to hear God's Word.

They liked to talk to God there.

And they liked to talk to God's people.

"They are a happy family," people said.

"They do good work with wood.

And they do good work for God, too."

something to ask

1. What work did Joseph do?

2. How did Jesus help him?

3. Do good helpers make happy families?

4. Are you a good helper?

5. How can you help your family to
   be happy?

something to do

Which of these will help your family be happy?

Which will not help your family be happy?

Jesus Pleases God

The Temptation of Christ, from Matthew 4

Jesus grew and became a man.

One day Jesus went away from his town.

He wanted to be alone.

Jesus talked to God for many days.

Then Satan came to see Jesus.

Jesus had not had food for a long time.

"You can make food from those rocks,"

Satan said. He was tempting Jesus.

315

But Jesus knew that he must not do
what Satan said.

"I must do what God tells me," said Jesus.

Satan asked Jesus three times to do
something that God would not like.

But Jesus would not do what Satan said.

"I must please God," Jesus told Satan.

Satan saw that he could

not get Jesus

to do what he wanted.

So Satan went away.

God was very pleased.

Jesus would not do what

Satan said.

something to ask

1. What did Satan want Jesus to do?

2. But what did Jesus do?

3. What kinds of things does Satan want you to do?

4. What should you do?

something to do

What should you do when you are tempted to do bad things?

Do what you want?

Ask a friend to help you?

Ask God to help you?

Ask Mother or
Father to help you?

God's House

Jesus Drives Out the Money-Changers, from John 2

Jesus liked to go to God's house.

He liked to talk to God there.

He liked to be with God's people.

But Jesus did not like

what some men were doing.

They were not talking with God.

They were not talking with God's people.

These men sold animals in God's house.

These men liked to cheat.

They liked to steal, too.

"You are not doing what you

should do

in God's house," Jesus said.

"You must get out!"

Jesus made these men

get out of God's house.

"God's house is not a place to cheat

and steal," said Jesus.

"We should go to God's house to

be with him.

We should talk to God in his house.

We should talk with God's people, too."

something to ask

1. What should people do in God's house?

2. What were the men doing there?

3. What did Jesus tell them to do?

4. What do YOU do when you go to God's house?

5. What should you do?

something to do

Who will you find in God's house?

God?

God's friends?

Your friends who love God?

Others who love God?

What Should I Do in God's House?

Jesus Reads from the Scriptures, from Luke 4

"Look who is here!" some people said.

All the people looked. Jesus was coming.

He was coming into God's house.

Jesus went up where the people could see him.

Then he looked at God's Word.

Jesus began to read what God's Word said.

The boys and girls were quiet.

The mothers and fathers were quiet, too.

Jesus told them about God's Son.

He told them what God's Word said about him.

"I am God's Son," he told them.

"No," some of the people said.

"You are not God's Son."

The people did not like what
Jesus said.

They took him away from God's
house. They tried to kill him.

But Jesus went away from them.

These people made Jesus sad.

They did not do what they
should with God's Son.

something to ask

1. What did Jesus do in God's house?

2. What did the people do?

3. What should people do with God's Son in God's house?

something to do

What things should you do in God's house?

A Friend Who Was Sick

Jesus Heals a Paralytic, from Mark 2

"Is Jesus in the house?" some men asked.

"Yes, but you cannot get in," said others.

"There are too many people."

"Our friend is sick," said the men,

"and Jesus can make him well."

But the men could not get into the house.

There were people here and
people there.
The men could not get through.
"Then we will go in another
way," they said.
So they let their friend down
through the roof.
"Please help our friend," they
said to Jesus. "He is sick."

Jesus was happy to help their sick friend.

"Get up," said Jesus. "You are well."

The man got up. He was not sick now.

He was so happy.

"Thank you! Thank you!" he said.

The men were happy, too.

Their friend did not hurt now.

Jesus had made him well.

something to ask

1. What did the sick man's friends do?

2. How did Jesus help?

3. How can Jesus help you when you hurt?

4. Will you ask him to help you?

something to do

What can you do for a friend when he hurts?

Which of these would you do?

Ask God to help him?

Tell him you are his friend?

Ask others to help him?

Tell him how bad he is?

Tell him how good you are?

Doing God's Work

Jesus Calls Matthew, from Matthew 9

Matthew had good work.

He had all the money he wanted.

And people did what he told them to do.

But Matthew was not happy.

He knew that he did not please God in his work.

One day Jesus came to see Matthew.

"Matthew," Jesus said,

"come with me and work for me."

Matthew looked at Jesus.

Jesus would not pay him for his work.

He would not make much money.

People would not do what he said.

He would have to do what Jesus said.

"What should I do?" Matthew asked.

Then Matthew knew.

He would please God if he

went with Jesus.

And he would be happy.

So Matthew went with Jesus.

He helped Jesus do God's work.

Then Matthew was very happy.

something to ask

1. Why was Matthew not happy?

2. What helped him become happy?

3. What can make YOU happy?

4. Will you do these things?

something to do

What will make you happy:

When you do what you want?

When you do what your friends tell you to do?

When you do what God wants?

When you do what Mother and Father ask you?

Look What Jesus Can do!

Jesus Stills a Storm, from Luke 8

"Come with me," said Jesus.

"Where?" asked his friends.

"To the other side of the lake," Jesus said.

Jesus and his friends got into their boat.

These friends liked to go with Jesus.

They knew that Jesus did good things for God.

They knew that God helped Jesus do these things.

Soon the boat was out on
the water.

Then the wind started to blow.

Faster and faster went the wind.

The boat went up and down on
the water.

Jesus' friends were so afraid.

"Help us!" they said to Jesus.

"The boat is going down!"

Jesus looked at the wind blowing on the water.

"Stop!" he said.

The wind stopped blowing.

The water stopped going up and down.

And the boat stopped going up and down.

"Did you see that?" one of Jesus' friends said.

The others looked at Jesus.

"Only God's Son could do that," they said.

something to ask

1. Who told the wind what to do?

2. How could he do that?

3. Do you know anyone who can do that?

4. Can you do that?

5. Do you do what Jesus wants, too?

something to do

Which of these should do what Jesus says to do?

Can a Man Do This?

Jesus Heals a Little Girl, from Mark 5

"Please come to my house," Jairus said.

"My little girl is going to die."

Jesus went with Jairus.

But it took a long time to get to his house.

People were here.

People were there.

The people all wanted to see Jesus.

Then someone came from
Jairus' house and said,
"Your little girl has died."
Jairus was so sad, but Jesus
said, "Don't be afraid."
Jesus and Jairus went into the
house. People were crying.
"Don't be sad," said Jesus.
"The little girl is sleeping."

Some people laughed at Jesus.

"Get out of this house," Jesus said to them.

So the people who laughed went away.

Jesus looked at the girl.

"Get up, little girl!" he said to her.

The little girl got up.

"Give her something to eat," said Jesus.

Jairus and the girl's mother were so happy.

"Can a man do this?" they asked.

"Jesus must be God's Son!"

something to ask

1. What did Jesus do for the girl?

2. Can a man do this?

3. Who is Jesus?

4. What book tells you about Jesus?

something to do

Which of these people did what Jesus said?

Jairus?

The little girl?

The people in
Jairus' house?

Do you?

A Boy Shares His Lunch

Jesus Feeds the Five Thousand, from Matthew 14

"Here are five pieces of bread

and two fish for your lunch," a mother said.

The boy was happy.

He was going to see Jesus.

So were some of his friends.

The boy took his lunch. He ran with his friends.

At last they saw Jesus.

There were many other people there, too.

371

Jesus said many good things.

The boy and his friends listened.

Then Jesus stopped talking.

Some men came to the boy.

"May we have your lunch?" they

asked. "Jesus wants it."

The boy took his lunch to Jesus.

He was happy to give Jesus

his lunch.

The boy and his friends watched.

But Jesus did not eat the lunch.

He broke it into many pieces.

He gave the pieces to the people.

Soon all the people had as much

to eat as they wanted.

Jesus smiled at the boy and his friends.

"Thank you for your lunch," he said.

The boy smiled, too.

Then he sat near Jesus and ate

some bread and fish.

something to ask

1. What was in the boy's lunch?

2. What did Jesus do with it?

3. Was the boy happy to share his
   lunch with Jesus?

4. Would you like to share something
   with Jesus?

something to do

What could you share with Jesus?

Talk with Mother or Father about this.

Walking on Water

Jesus Walks on the Sea of Galilee, from Mark 6

"It is time for you to go home," Jesus said.

"Will you come with us?" his friends asked.

"Not now," said Jesus.

Jesus' friends got into their boat.

They went out on the water to go home.

Soon it was night.

The wind began to blow hard.

The water went up and down.

They worked and worked to
get the boat home.

Suddenly all of them stopped.

"Look," they said.

"Who is that walking on
the water?"

The men were afraid.

"It is a ghost!" they said.

"No, I am not a ghost,"

the man on the water said.

"It is Jesus!" said his friends.

They were so happy that it was Jesus.

"But how can he do that?" someone asked.

"Only God's Son can do things like that,"

said others. "Jesus is God's Son."

something to ask

1. Can your friends walk on water?

2. Can you?

3. Who did walk on water?

4. How could he do this?

5. Do you love God's Son?

6. Will you talk to him now?

something to do

Did God make this?

And this?

And this?

What other work can he do?

What other things did he make?

God Talks about His Son

The Transfiguration of Christ, from Matthew 17

Jesus and some friends walked up and up and up.

They went up a tall mountain.

"Why are we here?" said one friend to the other.

"We do not know," he said, "but Jesus knows."

Then Jesus' face began to shine.

His clothes began to shine, too.

Jesus' friends were so afraid.

Then two men came to be with Jesus.

"Look at those men," said Jesus' friends.

"They lived a long time ago."

Then a big cloud came over all of them.

"This is my Son," someone said.

"Do what he says."

It was God who said this.

Jesus' friends were afraid,

so they fell down by Jesus.

When they got up,

there was no one there—

no one but Jesus.

"God said that,"

said Jesus' friends.

"God said that Jesus is his Son."

Now they knew that Jesus

was God's Son.

something to ask

1. What did God say about Jesus?

2. Who was with Jesus then?

3. What can you do to please Jesus?

4. Will you do one thing for Jesus soon?

something to do

Who said that Jesus was God's Son?

Jesus did.   So did his friends.   So did God.

What do you say?

A Man Who Did Not Say Thank You

The Parable of the Rich Fool, from Luke 12

There was a man who was very rich.

He had a farm. He had big barns.

He had houses. He had money.

The man had so many things!

He did not know what to do with all his things.

"I will make bigger barns," the man said.

"I will make them bigger and bigger."

The man loved his things

more than he loved God.

He did not thank God for them.

He did not give anything away.

"These are my things." he said.

"I want them all."

But God said, "It is time for

you to die. Then others will

have all your things."

The man did not like to hear this.

But what could he do?

That night he died.

Then others had all his things.

God gives us many good things.

We should give our love to him.

And we should thank him

for the things he gives to us.

something to ask

1. Was this man rich or poor?

2. Did he want to share his things?

3. What happened to the man?

4. What things did he take with him when he died?

something to do

How can you say thank you to God?

"Thank you for your good things."

"I will do my best for you."

"I will give good things to you."

"I will share with others."

"I will tell a friend about you."

"I will love you."

The Good Shepherd

The Parable of the Lost Sheep, from Luke 15

One day Jesus told his friends about a sheep.

It was a sheep that ran away.

The sheep went far away from the others.

It could not find the way home. It was lost!

The shepherd looked at
his sheep.

He saw that one sheep
was gone.

He loved that sheep,
and he wanted to find it.

So he left his other sheep.

He went far away from home
looking for his lost sheep.

The shepherd looked and looked

for his sheep. Then he found it.

The shepherd took the sheep into his arms.

Then he took the sheep to his home.

Jesus said that we are like the sheep.

We are far away from God.

But Jesus came to find us.

He loves us.

And he helps us find the way

to God's home in heaven.

something to ask

1. What did the sheep do?

   How did it get lost?

2. What did the shepherd do?

3. How are we like the sheep?

4. What does Jesus help us do?

something to do

How can you help your family to be happy?

Jesus and the Children

Children Come to Christ, from Mark 10

"What do you want?"

some of Jesus' friends asked.

"We want to have our children see Jesus,"

said the mothers and fathers.

"You cannot do that," said Jesus' friends.

"Why not?" asked the mothers and fathers.

"Jesus has too many things to do,"

said his friends. "That's why."

Then Jesus came to them.

"What is the matter?" he asked.

"Your friends will not let our children see you," said the mothers and fathers.

Jesus' friends said, "We told them that you were doing other things."

"Do not tell the children to stay away from me," said Jesus.

"They show others how to come to me."

Then Jesus had the children
come to see him.

He told them many things.

He told them how much
God loved them.

"Do you love us, too?"
the children asked.

"Yes," said Jesus.

"And I want you to love me."

something to ask

1. Did Jesus tell the children to go away?

2. Are children important to Jesus?

3. Does Jesus love children?
   How do you know?

4. How can you show Jesus that
   you love him?

something to do

Which kinds of children does Jesus love?

A Man Who Wanted to See

words to know

bring
most
once

Jesus Heals a Blind Man, from Luke 18

One day Jesus was going into a town.

A poor man sat by the road.

He wanted someone to help him.

The man could not see.

He could not work.

Then Jesus came by.

"Help me," the man said to Jesus.

"Help me! Help me! Help me!"

"Stop that!" some people said.

But the man did not stop.

"Have him come here," said Jesus.

So some men helped bring him to Jesus.

"What do you want?" Jesus asked.

"I want to see," said the man.

"Then you will see," said Jesus.

At once the man could see.

He was so happy.

He could see trees.

He could see people.

And he could see Jesus.

"Thank you!" the man said.

Then the man went with Jesus

to help him do his work.

He loved Jesus very much, and

he knew that Jesus loved him.

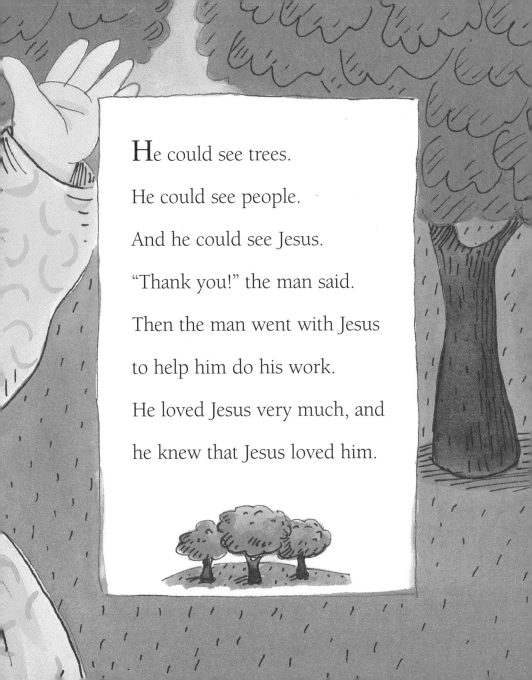

something to ask

1. What did the poor man want?

2. What did Jesus do for him?

3. Does Jesus love poor people?

4. How do you know?

5. Do you love poor people, too?

6. What can you do for them?

something to do

Which of these will help you most?

Which will make you the most happy?

Finding a Friend

Zacchaeus and Jesus, from Luke 19

Zacchaeus was sad. He wanted friends.

But no one wanted to be his friend.

"Zacchaeus cheats," some said.

"Zacchaeus steals," said others.

One day Zacchaeus saw Jesus.

"I want Jesus to be my friend," he said.

The people laughed. "Jesus is a good Man,"

they said. "He will not be your friend."

There were people all around Jesus.

Zacchaeus wanted to see Jesus.

But Zacchaeus was a little man.

He could not get through the crowds.

"I will climb that big tree and see Jesus," he said.

So Zacchaeus climbed the big tree.

Jesus stopped under the tree and looked up.

There was Zacchaeus.

"Come down," said Jesus.

"I want to go to your house.

I want to be your friend."

Zacchaeus was so happy.

He gave Jesus good things to eat.

"I'm sorry that I cheated," he said.

Jesus smiled at Zacchaeus.

"I forgive you," he said.

Zacchaeus was happy.

He had a new friend.

And Jesus is the best Friend of all.

something to ask

1. Why did Zacchaeus have no friends?

2. Who became his best friend?

3. Would you like Jesus to be your friend?
   Why?

something to do

Have you asked Jesus to be your friend?

Would you like to do that now?

Ask him to forgive you.

Ask him to help you please him.

Jesus on a Donkey

Christ Enters Jerusalem, from Mark 11

"I need a little donkey," said Jesus.

"It will help me do God's work."

Jesus' friends looked here. They looked there.

But they did not see a donkey.

"Where will we get a donkey?" they asked.

435

Jesus told his friends where to get a donkey.

He said a man would give them one.

Jesus' friends went to the man.

"May we use your donkey?" they asked.

"Yes," said the man. He was happy

that his donkey could help Jesus.

Then Jesus got on the donkey.

He went into a big town called Jerusalem.

Many people went with him to the big town.

They shouted, "Jesus is our King!"

In Jerusalem Jesus told people
about God.

He told them how to please God.

He told them that he would
die for them.

God had sent Jesus to do
these things.

This was the work Jesus did
for God.

something to ask

1. What kind of work did Jesus
   do for God?

2. How did the donkey help him?

3. What kind of work can you
   do for God?

something to do

How can these help you do God's work?

your   your   your

your   your

Supper with Jesus

The Lord's Supper, from Matthew 26

"Where will we eat?" Jesus' friends asked.

Jesus told them where it would be.

They would eat at a house in Jerusalem.

So Jesus' friends went there.

They put the supper together.

Then Jesus and his twelve friends ate together.

"Eat this bread," Jesus said. "When I am gone,

you will do this again and again.

Then you will think of the way I died for you."

Jesus' friends ate the bread.

But they were sad.

They did not want Jesus to die.

"Drink from this cup," Jesus said.

"When I am gone, you will do this

again and again. Then you will think

of the way I died for you."

Jesus' friends drank from the cup. But they were sad.

They did not want Jesus to die.

Suddenly the friends heard someone singing. It was Jesus.

Jesus' friends began to sing, too. This was a special time because Jesus was so special.

something to ask

1. Who was eating together?

2. What did Jesus give his friends? Why?

3. Who was singing?

something to do

When do you think of this special supper?

Talk with Mother or Father about this.

The Love of Jesus

The Death of Christ, from Matthew 27

"Nail that man to the cross!" someone said.

The men nailed Jesus to the cross.

Then they watched him die.

Jesus had not hurt these men.

But they were hurting him.

Jesus talked to God about these men.

"Forgive them for hurting me," he said.

These people had not seen a man like this.

They were hurting him.

But he was loving them.

"That man is God's Son," said one of them.

453

When Jesus died on the cross,

he showed how much he

loved them.

And he showed how much he

loves you and me.

How much does Jesus love us?

He loves us so much that he

died so we can come to God.

something to ask

1. Why did the men hurt Jesus?

2. Did he hurt them?

3. Did he love them?

4. Does Jesus love you?
   Does he forgive you?

5. Do you love him?

6. Would you like to tell him this?

something to do

How can you show Jesus that you love him?

How can you show it with each of these?

Jesus Is Alive Again!

Mary Sees the Risen Christ, from John 20

Mary was so sad.

Some men had killed Jesus.

Now Mary came to see where they had put him.

But Jesus was not there.

"Someone has taken him away," said Mary.

Mary began to cry.

Then some angels talked to Mary.

"Why are you crying?" they asked.

"Someone has taken Jesus away,"
she said.

Then Mary saw a man coming.

"Why are you crying?" he asked.

"Someone has taken Jesus away,"
she said.

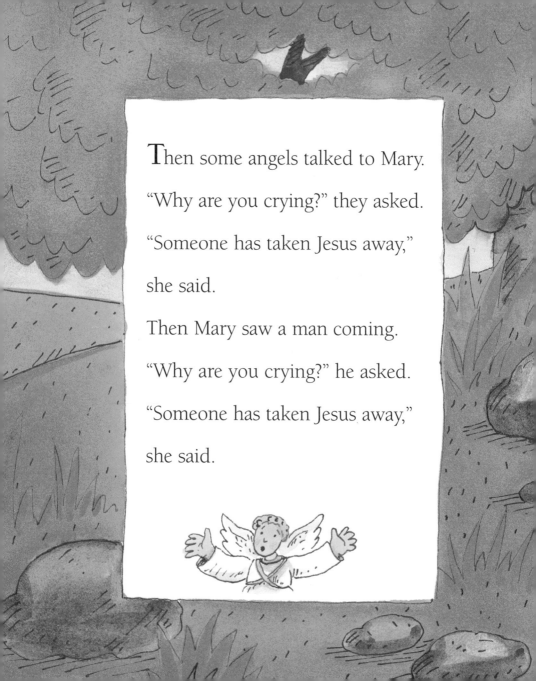

"Mary!" the man said.

"Jesus!" said Mary.

Mary was so happy.

Jesus was alive again!

"I cannot stay with you," Jesus said.

"I must go back to my home in heaven."

Now Mary knew that Jesus was God's Son.

something to ask

1. Why did Mary cry?

2. Who came to see her?

3. What did he tell Mary?

4. Who is Jesus?

5. How did Mary know that Jesus was God's Son?

something to do

How do you know that Jesus is God's Son?

He did God's work.

He told others about God.

He did not do bad things.

He helped some people come

alive after they died.

He said that he was God's Son.

He came alive after some men killed him.

Telling Others about Jesus

The Church Grows, from Acts 1-8

"Go to all the world," Jesus said.

"Tell people everywhere

about what I did for them."

After Jesus said these things

he went back to heaven to stay.

Jesus' friends knew that he was God's Son.

He had died for them.

Then he had come back to live with them.

Only God's Son could do that!

They knew that Jesus showed people

the way to know God.

So they went to all the people.

They went to tell them about Jesus.

469

"Jesus loves you," they said.

"He wants to help you get to know God."

Some people liked what they heard. But others said,

"Go away"

Jesus' friends were happy when some people did come to love Jesus.

something to ask

1. What did Jesus ask his friends to do?

2. How did they do it?

3. Why did they do it?

4. What does he want you to do for him?

5. How can you tell others about him?

something to do

Where should you tell others about Jesus?

At your house?

At a friend's house?

Here and there
and everywhere?

A Man Hears about Jesus

Philip and the Ethiopian, from Acts 8

"Leave this town," an angel told Philip.

"Go where I tell you to go."

Philip left that town.

He went far away to the place

where the angel told him to go.

"But there are no people here," said Philip.

"How can I do God's work here?"

Then Philip saw a man coming.

The man was looking at God's

Word. "Do you know what it

says?" Philip asked.

"No," said the man. "I need

someone to help me.

Will you help me?"

"Yes," said Philip, "I will."

"God sent me here to help you."

So Philip told the man

what God's Word said.

He told the man about Jesus.

"I want to do what Jesus says,"

the man told Philip.

Philip was so happy.

Now he knew why God had sent him there.

He knew that this man

would tell many others about Jesus.

something to ask

1. What did the man want Philip to help him do?

2. Why do you want others to help you know God's Word?

3. Who can you help? What can you do to help them?

4. What can you do to know more about God's Word?

something to do

Where do you hear about Jesus?

God's Word?

Books about Jesus?

Mother
and Father?

God's house?

Friends who
love Jesus?

Brighter than the Sun

Saul's Conversion, from Acts 9

Saul hated Jesus.

And he hated Jesus' friends.

He did not want people to follow Jesus.

Saul did not think that Jesus was God's Son.

Saul thought Jesus was dead. He said,

"Why should people follow a dead person?"

So Saul tried to hurt Jesus' friends.

One day Saul went to a city
called Damascus.
He went to hurt Jesus' friends.
But on the way, something
happened.
Suddenly the sky was bright.
It was brighter than the sun.
It was so bright that Saul fell
down.

Then someone from heaven said,

"Stop hurting me."

"Who are you?" Saul asked.

"What do you want me to do?"

He was afraid. No one from heaven

had talked to him before.

"I am Jesus," the person said. "Follow me!"

Now Saul knew that Jesus was alive.

He knew that Jesus was God's Son.

He knew that Jesus was in heaven.

He would follow Jesus as long as he lived.

something to ask

1. Why did Saul hate Jesus' friends?

2. What did he want them to do?

3. Why did he go to Damascus?

4. Who talked to him?
   What did Jesus say?

5. Why did Saul become Jesus' follower?

something to do

Have you asked Jesus,

"What would you like me to do for you?"

Would you like to ask him now?

Singing in Jail

Paul and Silas in Prison, from Acts 16

Paul and Silas were doing God's work.

They were telling people that Jesus is God's Son.

They were helping people love Jesus.

But some men did not like that.

They hated Jesus. They hated Jesus' friends, too.

"Put those men in jail!" they shouted.

"They are doing bad things."

Some men put Paul and Silas in jail. That night Paul and Silas began to sing songs about God. Suddenly the jail began to shake. The door of the jail broke. The man at the jail was afraid that someone would hurt him if Paul and Silas got away. So he tried to kill himself.

"Stop," said Paul. "We are all here."

Now the man knew that God took care

of Paul and Silas.

"I want Jesus to forgive me," he said.

"I want to love Jesus and follow him.

What should I do?"

"Ask Jesus to forgive you," said Paul

So the man did. He prayed to Jesus.

His family became Jesus' friends, too.

They were all happy.

Do you think they sang happy songs, too?

something to ask

1. Why did men put Paul and
   Silas in jail?

2. What did they do in jail?

3. What do you do when you get hurt?
   Do you sing, or do you say bad things?

4. What good thing happened to the
   man at the jail?

something to do

When should we sing songs about God?

When things go well?

When people hurt me?

When people help me?

When I am happy?

When I am not happy?

Paul Is a Brave Helper

Paul's Shipwreck, from Acts 27

"What can we do?" the people cried.

The wind made their boat go here and there.

The rain came down on them.

They were in a bad storm.

There was nothing they could do.

"We will all be killed!" they said.

"No," said Paul, "God told me that no one will be killed."

Then Paul told them about God. He told them how God would help them.

Paul was very brave.

He knew that God was with them.

The storm made the boat

sink under the water.

But the people did not go down with it.

God helped them get to the land.

Then the people were happy that

Paul was with them.

They were happy that he was

God's brave helper.

something to ask

1. What did Paul do when a storm came?

2. How was he brave when others were afraid?

3. How was this doing God's work?

4. How can you be brave when others are afraid?

something to do

How are these people helping others

who are afraid?

Helping a Friend

Paul and Onesimus, from the Book of Philemon

Onesimus had run away.

Onesimus had worked for Philemon.

But he had run away from Philemon.

Onesimus had taken some

of Philemon's things, too.

Onesimus ran away to a big town.

Paul saw Onesimus in the big town. He told him about Jesus. Onesimus began to love Jesus. Then he wanted to go back home to Philemon.

He wanted Philemon to take him back.

He wanted Philemon to love him and not hurt him.

510

So Paul wrote to Philemon for Onesimus.

"Philemon," Paul said,

"Onesimus loves Jesus now.

He wants to do what is right.

Will you take him back to work for you?"

Onesimus was happy to have a friend like Paul.

He was happy that Paul helped him do

what was right.

something to ask

1. What did Onesimus do?

2. Why did he want to go back to Philemon?

3. How did Paul help Onesimus?

4. What do you think Philemon did?

5. How can you help others do what they should for God?

something to do

How can you help a friend do what is right?

Talk to him?

Make fun of him?

Work with him?

Tell others bad things about him?

Ask God to help him?

Story List

Basic Words List

Most of the 250 words on this basic word list have come from standard word lists used in public school early reader books. If your child is learning to read in a public or private school, he or she should be familiar with most of these basic words. This will depend, of course, on the specific school reading materials used.

   With each Bible story reading you will find no more than five new words not found on the basic list. These new words are accumulated so that a new word used in one reading never appears as a new word in subsequent readings.

a	be	does	give	into	make
about	became	don't	go	is	man
across	become	done	gone	it	many
afraid	been	down	good	jump	may
after	began	each	got	keep	me
again	being	eat	had	kept	mean
ago	best	every	happen	kill	men
all	better	everyone	happy	kind	more
am	big	fall	has	king	mother
an	boat	far	have	knew	much
and	boy	fast	he	know	must
animal	but	father	hear	last	my
another	buy	feel	help	laugh	name
any	by	fell	her	lead	near
are	call	find	here	led	neat
around	came	fish	him	let	never
as	can	food	his	lie	new
ask	children	for	home	like	night
at	come	friend	house	little	no
ate	could	from	how	live	not
away	cut	fun	hurt	long	now
baby	day	gave	I	look	of
back	did	get	if	love	on
bad	do	girl	in	made	one

only	saw	song	there	until	who
or	say	soon	these	up	why
other	sea	stay	they	us	will
our	see	steal	thing	very	wind
out	seen	step	this	walk	with
over	sell	stop	those	want	women
people	send	surprise	threw	was	won
play	sent	take	through	wash	word
please	she	talk	throw	water	work
put	should	tall	time	way	would
rain	shout	tell	to	we	write
ran	show	than	told	well	yes
road	sing	thank	too	went	you
run	so	that	took	were	your
sad	some	the	town	what	
said	someone	their	tree	when	
sang	something	them	tried	where	
sat	son	then	try	which	

New Words List

The following is a cumulative list of the new words used in the Bible readings. No more than five new words are used in any story, and usually a smaller number is used.

Because these stories are from the Bible, many of the new words are names of Bible people or places. These words are first steps in acquainting your child with the people and places of the Bible.

Abraham	angry	barn	Bethlehem	box	bring
Adam	anymore	basket	Bible	brass	broke
alive	anyone	beautiful	bird	brave	brother
alone	arm	because	Boaz	bread	build
angel	arrow	belong	bow	bright	burn

continued...

bush	everywhere	Jacob	Moses	river	stone
calf	face	jail	most	robe	storm
camel	family	Jairus	mountain	rock	strong
cannot	farm	Jericho	Naaman	roof	suddenly
care	fight	Jerusalem	nail	room	sun
carpenter	fill	Jesus	Naomi	rule	supper
cheat	fire	Joash	need	Ruth	surprise
city	five	Job	Nehemiah	Samson	swallow
climb	fix	Jonah	Nineveh	Samuel	sword
cloth	follow	Jonathan	Noah	Sarah	tempt
clothes	forgive	Joseph	nothing	Satan	thought
cloud	found	Joshua	obey	Saul	three
count	ghost	kitchen	once	seven	thunder
cross	gift	ladder	Onesimus	shake	together
crowd	God	lake	paper	share	tore
cry	gold	land	Paul	sheep	turn
cup	Goliath	law	pay	shepherd	TV
Damascus	grain	learn	person	shine	twelve
Daniel	grew	leave	Philemon	shout	two
David	grow	left	Philip	sick	under
dead	hand	leprosy	piece	side	use
die	Hannah	lightning	place	Silas	wall
donkey	happen	lion	poor	sink	watch
door	hard	listen	pray	sky	wife
drank	hate	lost	princess	slave	wise
dream	heard	lunch	promise	sleep	women
drink	heaven	manna	punish	sling	wood
dry	hide	Mary	queen	smile	world
Egypt	high	matter	quiet	snake	wrote
Eli	himself	Matthew	rainbow	sold	Zacchaeus
Elijah	hungry	means	read	Solomon	
Elisha	husband	Miriam	rest	sorry	
Esther	important	money	rich	special	
Eve	Isaac	moon	right	stars	